Angel
ON MY SHOULDER

The Flying Kid

KEITH BOWES

ANGEL ON MY SHOULDER
Copyright © 2017 by Keith Bowes

Printed in Canada

ISBN: 978-1-4866-1458-5

Word Alive Press
131 Cordite Road, Winnipeg, MB R3W 1S1
www.wordalivepress.ca

Library and Archives Canada Cataloguing in Publication

Bowes, Keith, 1926-, author
    Angel on my shoulder : the flying kid / Keith Bowes.

Issued in print and electronic formats.
ISBN 978-1-4866-1458-5 (softcover).--ISBN 978-1-4866-1459-2 (ebook)

    1. Bowes, Keith, 1926-. 2. Air pilots--Religious life--Canada.
3. Air pilots--Canada--Biography. 4. Christian biography--Canada.
I. Title.

BR1725.B6885A3 2017   270.092   C2017-901774-8
                                                  C2017-901775-6

Contents

CHAPTER ONE

Earliest Memories

K B. That's what I've been called all my life. KB, that's me

My first memory of anything in this world is listening from an upstairs bedroom, hearing good, old-time music drifting up the stairway at this old farmhouse where Dad and Mom were at a country dance. Dad would be down there playing the banjo, Uncle George would be on the violin, someone else would be playing on a piano, and in the background you would hear people dancing, talking, laughing, and so on. To me there is no better sound than that, and it's still stamped in my head today.

From my early days, I also remember that I had the bad habit of following right at the heels of old Dolly, an old grey mare from Dad's herd. Dolly didn't like this at all, and decided to give me a good swift kick in the face—the front tip of her hoof caught me just between my right eye and eyebrow. The scar is still there 87 years later. A close call. If that hoof had landed half an inch lower I wouldn't have an eye. I can't help but think that my "Angel" made sure that it didn't happen. How do you thank an angel enough?

It seems that I didn't learn my lesson from her first kick, so Dolly, like a good teacher, remedied that shortly afterward by giving me another really solid kick, square in my face. I'm sure she figured that little three-year-old boy wouldn't forget this time. The result was a flat face; Mom said I was unrecognizable because of the mass of blood and dirt. But thanks again, Angel, because it could have been a lot worse.

The next incident was a little while later. As far as I can remember I was four years old, maybe five, but it was before I started school. Dad had his outfit at a neighbour's farm, custom threshing. There were about three or four grain wagons, each with a team of horses, to take the grain from the threshing machine to the grainery at the farmyard. There would always be one, two or three wagons waiting in line to pull up under the grain spout of the thresher, where they would be loaded.

It must have been pretty tiring for a little boy hanging around a threshing outfit on a hot, lazy summer day. Accordingly, I decided a little siesta was in order. So I snuck into one of the wagons waiting in line to be loaded. The clean, flat floor in its grain box was the only place in the threshing outfit where a guy could lie down and catch a little sleep.

When that grain wagon's turn to be loaded came, it pulled up under the grain spout and started filling up. About this time, Dad suddenly realized that Keith wasn't anywhere to be found. I'm quite sure he was the one who thought to look into the wagon box that was filling up with grain.

There I was, lying on the floor of the grain box. They say the grain was already creeping over me, but I was having a nice sound sleep. A few more minutes and I would have become a statistic. I'm convinced that Angel had a hand in not letting it happen. So again, many, many thanks, Angel.

In the next incident, I had just started going to school, which would put me at five years old. We were playing softball and I was next up to bat, waiting for a big boy to finish his turn. He had a queer habit of continuing the swing right around behind himself whenever he missed the ball. There I was, standing right at his shirt tail—talk about anxious. Anyhow, he missed the ball and continued his swing right around behind him, and hit me with his bat on the left side of my face really hard.

One of the big boys loaded me up on the back of his horse and buggy. On the way home I remember waking up for a second or so—he had that horse and buggy in overdrive. Next thing, I was conscious again, and Mom's face was almost in mine, yelling at me, "Wake up, wake up." We lived a mile and a half from the school. He had come roaring into the yard, yelling at Mom, "I've got your boy." I'd been unconscious for almost an hour, I recall Mom saying. For a little head to come through that hard a blow without a concussion or some other major problem, I think Angel deserves credit yet again.

I also recall an incident by our big swing at school. It was a very high double swing set—twelve to fourteen feet. Two kids would stand on a 2 x 6 seat facing each other, and the contest would be on to see which pair could pump up their swing the highest. Some kids could get the swing up over the top level, which was darn high.

I was running at top speed—probably playing tag or something—and apparently not carefully watching where I was going, because I carelessly cut across the path of the swing. They were just coming down and the seat nailed me on the left side around the cheek.

The teacher said I was unconscious for about twenty minutes; again when I came to, I remember the teacher's face, right in mine, saying, "Wake up, wake up Keith," Again I'm truly thankful that my head survived another big blow without major injury. And again I'm convinced Angel had an influence, so once more, thanks Angel.

I'm holding my favourite flying model airplane out of all the models I built. I'm sure this hobby was what drew me into flying. This model plane was astonishing: it was light in weight, and had a powerful rubber band motor driving the very large propeller. Boy, could it fly!

CHAPTER TWO

Adventures on the Farm

It's time to move to the stage where I became of some use in the world. I distinctly remember being seven years old when Dad first took me to the barn to do chores—somewhere between 6 and 7 AM—and taught me the art of milking a cow as I was sitting on a little milking stool with the milk pail between my legs.

Let me tell you, there is a science to the operation. You gently put your hand around the cow's teat and wrap your fingers around it. Next you start closing your hand, starting with the first finger, then the second, third, and fourth. By now you will have squeezed some milk out of the teat, and the cow will be quite content if you have done this gently but firmly. If you keep up this gentle and steady operation, you should end up with a fair amount of milk in the pail.

Now, not every milking operation goes as smoothly as what I've just described. For instance, maybe the old cow had walked through a barbed wire fence that day, figuring the grass was greener on the other side. Many times, the cow had torn up her bag and teats pretty bad. But if there was only a minor cut or two, you still had the job of getting the milk into the pail.

Once in a while, the old cow got fed up with the ordeal. I've often marveled at how that old cow could take a quick look, and then suddenly, with extreme accuracy, lift her leg up and put it down smack into the milk pail, and then, with the force of a mule, kick bucket, stool and this boy across to the other side of the aisle. Sometimes I landed right behind the horses' feet. Now that's a place I didn't want to spend much time, so I scrambled out of there fast as possible before getting re-launched back to the cow's side.

You can imagine the trail of milk on the floor from all this commotion. Every cat on the farm would be there, lapping and licking like mad.

Now we shift to the pigs. To set the stage: Dad had taken the threshing machine down to the slough to create an extra big straw pile. He had a long, heavy rod, with a harpoon point on one end and a ring on the other. He then pushed the harpoon spear deep into the straw stack with the tractor, close to the ground. After pulling the harpoon rod out with the tractor, the result was a crude narrow tunnel at ground level, going right to the centre of the pile.

It didn't take the pigs long to start nosing into there. It was winter and they found that nice, warm tunnel very cozy. So they kept on nosing deeper into the pile. At the end of the tunnel they made a room, which was their residence from then on. From my recollection, Dad must have had a half dozen to a dozen pigs in stock each year.

Sometimes, I actually crawled through the tunnel right into their room. It was not too often, because I had to be certain that there were no pigs inside—not even one or two. When the pigs decided to exit their tunnel, it was similar to a bullet train; they were in high gear. Can you think of anything more suicidal than being in that tight spot when the pigs were coming out? I think Angel had tight control over the whole pig scenario. Thanks again, Angel, thanks!

The chickens are the next chapter in these ramblings about the life of a young farm boy in the 1930s, an era when the economy of a farming family was almost cashless. The only two items that actually brought in cash to our family were crates of eggs and cans of cream which the truck would pick up. The rest was bartering—mostly firewood to Campbell's grocery store for flour and other groceries Mom needed to cook and bake all our food from scratch. The local farmers had a "beef ring," where each participant took their turn to butcher an animal and divide up the meat between the other members.

And as for the cream, I'll never forget turning the cream separator handle for forty-five minutes every night, seven days a week, in order to have "x" number of cream cans for the local truck to pick up. If you ever want to know how long forty-five minutes can be, turn a cream separator handle for three quarters of an hour.

Then there were the egg crates that Mom and Dad had to fill for pickup by the truck. This scenario brings to mind one of the games we played, this one in the hen house.

A neighbour boy and I would enter the hen house, where Dad usually had between forty and sixty laying hens. Our contest would be to see which one of us could get the most chickens lined up asleep with their heads tucked under their wings. The challenge was to catch the chicken, tuck its head under its wing, and rock it back and forth until it went to sleep. We would each put our sleeping chickens in our own rows. Chickens will only stay asleep so long, so we had to work fast. But you can imagine how dusty and full of feathers the atmosphere was in that old hen house.

Anyhow, those sessions were hard on egg production, as chickens were flying all over the place very disrupted. Dad never outright forbade us to play this game, but he came pretty close, because upon looking back it must have cut down the income for egg sales, which meant less cash for purchasing.

The hen house calls to mind another very dusty atmosphere—one many times worse. Dad had built the grainery, which held all our grain production until the elevator could take it in. Our grainery was actually a small elevator itself. It had a "leg" coming up the centre of the building—a long, large belt with grain cups riveted to it—which carried the grain from the bottom of the incoming grain pit, to the top of the building, where it was then collected and directed to one of the four bins surrounding the elevation leg system.

All this grain movement produced incredible amounts of dust. There were only two small windows at the top of the grainery, which barely helped with the dirty air. Eventually the bin would fill up to the tip of the spout, after which someone had to get right into the bin and start shoveling the incoming grain into the corners until the bin was full and level. There was a little square window at the east gable, almost at the peak. You could barely see the light of daylight from it due to the dusty air. When the bin finally got shoveled level full to the corners, you could go outside.

I can still recall hacking up pure black solid oysters for hours after leaving the grainery. How my lungs came through those ordeals and are still working is a bit of a mystery. We did put wet handkerchiefs over our noses, just like a highway bandit, which helped a bit, but I'm convinced that my Angel had a hand in getting me through it OK. Thanks again, Angel.

Dad built the barn in 1933 from our own lumber. He had set up a sawmill at the slough, and hauled logs up from the bush. He hired a carpenter to supervise the project. They made everything they needed—even the rafters. The barn is now more than eighty years old, and it still stands just as straight and erect as the day they built it.

Dad kept the horses and the other livestock in the barn that first winter. Later, he emptied it out and white-washed the bottom part, laid down a hardwood dance floor in the loft, and started the "Bowes Barn Dances" to bring in much-needed cash. It worked. "Bowes Barn Dances" became the place to go. Dad hosted a barn dance every week, and sometimes two. He kept horses and the livestock in the barn for the winter, and then dances in the summer.

Every dance band in the country played in the barn – Dema's Serenaders, Walter Mahon, Andy Desjarlis & His Early Settlers, Fred Hydaller & His Alberta Cowgirls, Art McQuing & the Farmer Fiddlers, Jimmy Gowler, and many more. In later years, Glen Frain & His Buckaroos became a weekly event. For every dance in over twenty years, Dad bought a big box of doughnuts from Fuller's bakery and Mom made a big tub of coffee, and at midnight everybody had a feast of free doughnuts and coffee—boy, were they good. But to feed three hundred to five hundred people it took a huge quantity.

When Dad put the animals back in the barn for the winter, he also filled the loft with hay. One load comprised three slings of hay hoisted up by a long rope to a pulley at the peak of the barn, where two big doors opened up to let the slings in one at a time. The rope ran along a rail that went to the back wall and out a hole to a team of horses that pulled the rope.

I'm not overly proud of this next caper—if there was any boyish devilment in me, this is one of the times it came out. I sweet-talked my young sister into sitting on a sling, after the hay was dumped out of it. The sling was just like a big swing, and it had a rope tied to it so I could pull her from one end of the loft to the other. As I pulled her along back and forth, the trips got gradually faster and faster, until I was pulling her as fast as I could. What I did, of course, was to stop just short of slamming into the end of the barn, and she swung right up to within a few feet of the walls.

Well, Mom heard her terrified screams from the house. She came out to the barn loft as fast as she could to lay down the law, telling me to get out of that loft and never do that again. But I know it happened a lot more than once.

I can see now that I gave Mom a pretty hard time. I might as well relate to you another nasty little game that I pulled off a few times with my sister. The hens would get up on the top of the straw pile in the slough and lay eggs all over the place. I would throw the eggs from the top of the pile toward a certain spot on the ground where my sister was gathering them. I had in mind I could play the part of Mr. Innocent if an egg happened to splatter on her leather helmet. But when it happened and she went running up to the house with egg running down everywhere, bawling, Mom came storming down to the slough and demanded that I get down from that straw pile right now, and never go up there again. I don't think she bought into the Mr. Innocent thing. Mom was a very unhappy camper. Looking back on these events, I don't think I could claim to have been the perfect farm boy, growing up on a pretty active farm.

I haven't touched on what happened with the horses yet. Dad had three main teams that he harnessed up to the large implements—the seeding drill, cultivator, etc. Nellie and Mable were his number one team, Jean and Judy were a younger second team, and I can't recall the names of the third.

What I do remember distinctly was that Nellie had lost her left eye through some accident or mishap, and as a result she was extremely hyperactive. I can remember having to go up into her stall on her right side, probably to give her some oats. She would start jumping around and stamping her hooves on the floor like mad. I was always afraid she would stomp on my feet, but she never did. In all her jumping and stomping she would crush you against the stall wall, not hard enough to hurt you but enough to inform you that she didn't want you there. She was a pretty smart old horse. I also remember that when you were passing by her manger in the alleyway in front of her, you had to look right into her good eye all the time you were within her reach. If you forgot to do so, you received a horse bite in your rump. And, let me tell you, if you ever received one you wouldn't forget it soon.

Dad building his barn in 1933, where he held the Bowes barn dances for 20 years, until 1953. Constructed from lumber sawed by his own saw mill, using logs cut from the south end of our farm, down by the river.

CHAPTER THREE

Teenage Years

At the age of fourteen or fifteen, Mom and Dad took me to the family doctor, and he diagnosed me with four diseases: rheumatic fever, St Vitus Dance, nervous breakdown and heart murmur! He said, "That boy has to go to bed for eight or nine months." I lay in bed from early fall until the next spring, becoming weaker and weaker. I remember that when I rolled over in bed, my heart would just speed up like a trip hammer.

However, the second day I was up in bed, Dad caught me a little grey baby rabbit, and BunBun grew up with me as his mother through the winter. He would lie beside me as close as he could get—I was fearful of rolling over on him, but it never happened—and soon grew to over a foot and a half long.

In May, Dad started encouraging me to go sit outside. One day he just picked me up and carried me out to a chair he had placed under the trees between the barn and the hen house. The bunny hopped along behind us, and all afternoon I enjoyed the fresh air with BunBun circling the chair, only venturing forty to fifty feet away and then back. He was exploring the yard. The next day Dad carried me out again from the room upstairs, and BunBun came along, but this time he explored further away, getting closer to the slough. Before the afternoon was over he made one big circle, stood up very straight and looked back at me for a while, and then turned towards the slough and hopped away.

I never saw him again. He had said "Goodbye" as the wild took over. BunBun had been my buddy and I had been his mother! He had really helped me get through the winter.

I had missed a year of classes, so I started back in grade eight at Nairn School. As I walked to school with my sisters, the other kids spotted us coming a quarter mile down the road and ran out to greet us. It was a good feeling to be welcomed back. That year consisted of resuming our little "World Series" at recess and noon hour, when we would form teams. We, the pitchers, had the first choice and would always select the good hitters. In the winter it was the same thing with hockey, always the best scorers.

We did a lot of kite flying back then. In those days, Dad was still using horses for field work, so there were always lots of bamboo whips—broken but with lots of the material left—for making the cross, then binder twine for the perimeter, brown paper, and a turkey cord for the sling and tail, which was made by taking a bunched up piece of brown paper and tying it in the middle and making a bow every foot. If the kite was about three feet long top to bottom the tail would be about twelve feet long.

I'll never forget when I made my biggest kite. It was about eight feet tall, a monster, so it had a tail of at least twenty feet long. I had underestimated the power of that kite. Even though I had found a line heavier than turkey cord, it still couldn't withstand the pulling power in the wind, so down she came tail first—it was quite a sight. Kite and tail together, it was almost thirty feet long.

It came down smack dab in the centre of the westbound lane, and wouldn't you know it, a woman was going west in the same lane. It was falling fast, so she never saw it until it fell on that highway, standing straight up, directly in front of her so that she ran smack right into it. Because it had dropped out of the sky right in front of her car, she almost had a heart attack. Well, when she got stopped and got out of the car, she was madder than a wet hen—I think that was the worst blast I ever got in my life! There was no real damage to her car, given the kite's construction materials. But, anyhow, I never flew my giant again.

Another favourite activity of mine was rafting in the slough. In those days, it would really fill up in the spring. Dad had gotten a bunch of big timbers when he built his saw mill, and there were two left over, a smaller one about 8" x 24" x 20' and a bigger one about 8" x 24" x 30'. So we got them into the water and they both made good rafts. We got our sea legs after falling off many times, and with poles we could propel both around pretty well. Then the battle was on—one would get on each and the idea was to ram the other guy and knock him off into the water. It was pretty deep—about three feet in the center of the slough.

One day a pal and I came up with an idea that we thought would be funny. Dad came walking out of the yard to the north field. He was going to get across by the road to the east, but we talked him into taking a ride across the water on our rafts. When we reached the middle of the slough we thought it would be hilarious if the raft started rocking and he fell into the water where it was deepest. Well, the big timber started rocking and rolling and he did fall off, and he certainly didn't think it was funny. He never crossed with us again.

We played one game that he simply wouldn't accept. We dreamed up a plan to go down to the slough and catch about a half dozen toads and frogs, and let them loose in the loft of the barn onto the dance floor. Then we would bring up our wagon, one of us pushing the other guy as fast as we could, and catch up to a toad or frog and squash it with the front wheel. It was really fun and challenging, as these frogs and toads were jumping all over the place. It took a while, as they were quick and fast.

But this created a big problem for Dad. It didn't matter how hard you tried, you could never get rid of that sticky spot where the frog or toad had been run over. So at the next barn dance, people's feet would come to an abrupt stop when they stepped on these spots. Then they would hunt down Dad and really raise a fuss.

Poor Dad. That was too much. After a good reprimand he told us straight out that we weren't going to play that game anymore—or else.

Let me tell one more story before I close off this era. We grew up on a very well-organized and operated family farm. I feel very fortunate. Dad and Mom ran things really well.

But on with my sad tale of woe. We boys had organized a game of hockey on the slough over at a neighbour's place. We were playing our big game when my sister showed up to skate around with us. Well, seeing as we were playing hockey, that wasn't possible, so she started skating around, just to the south of us.

That didn't last too long. Her skate soon got caught in a crack and she fell on her face, hitting her mouth on the ice. Not surprisingly, she bled and cried as she skated home.

Maybe I should have dropped out of the hockey game and went home with her, but at the time I didn't see what I could do to help. It wasn't far; she could skate to school every day and the school was one and a half miles from out house.

So I kept on with our hockey game. You wouldn't believe how seriously we took the sports we played, whether hockey or ball.

Anyhow, Dad took a completely different point of view, no doubt hearing my sister's side of the story. When I got home at supper time, all he said was, "You should have come home with your sister. She broke her front tooth."

He grabbed the long razor strap and gave me a strapping, the only one he ever gave me. I didn't forget it anytime soon, as those big straps really stung on a bare bum. I must say, I felt completely innocent, but that didn't cut any ice. But as time passed, it all went away. Time cures all, they say.

The finished Bowes barn and the Tiger Moth that I learned acrobatics with.
It was a fully acrobatic aircraft. A good airplane.

CHAPTER FOUR

I Start Flying

Next came high school at Portage Collegiate, where I completed grades nine and ten and began grade eleven. However, after nine days our math teacher was replaced, and I didn't care for the new one's method. As math was my main subject, I decided to quit school and get a job.

I started by "busting up frozen ground" with a pick axe at the Texaco bulk station for two weeks. Then a friend who drove a service truck for aircraft got me a job at the airport as a tow bar technician, which meant we rode around on a tractor hitch, pulling two tow bars which had two hooks welded onto the tow bars. We had to drop them into two rings which were welded on at the wheels of the aircraft, allowing us to tow the aircraft. We were responsible for getting the airplanes to the flight line, then putting them back in the hangar after the flight exercise. There were three shifts – days, evenings and graveyard (midnight til 8 AM).

A pilot at Southport was rebuilding a little Taylor Craft airplane – identification CF-BIE. He had the aircraft mostly rebuilt. I bought it from him for $800.oo, and that's when Dad built the hangar for us to work on it. It had the fabric on it but we had to dope it (apply weatherproof lacquer) and put the lettering and colours on. We worked on it for months. CF-BIE became the plane I flew after learning to fly at Aircraft Services Winnipeg.

I finally earned my Department of Transportation C. of A. saying the aircraft was airworthy to fly. My Taylorcraft, registered as CF-BIE, had one magneto (not the usual two), no flaps, no brakes, and no flying instruments except for an altimeter and a bubble on a curved concave level. The airspeed indicator was a paddle on a spring attached to a wing strut. All you had after that was the seat of your pants!

Every chance I got, I took the Taylorcraft up for a little fly around. I had the habit of flying really low, which did not overly impress one of our neighbours. I recall one time flying east, along the south side of the highway, and I happened to look down at the ground right under me. At that moment, I was flying over our first neighbour's yard. It turned out that this farmer was in the egg business. The yard was full of chickens, and they were flying around all over the yard like a bomb had gone off. Nearly a month later, the neighbour came to our house and told Dad that the hens hadn't laid an egg for three weeks after the flyover. He was not a happy camper.

The next low-flying incident was almost a heart-stopper—literally. I was coming back from Portage, flying east on the south side of the highway. Just as I was directly over the CNR tracks crossing, right out of the blue there was a sudden, extremely shrill screech. It was the loudest sound I'd ever heard, and hopefully ever will hear. I was directly over the train whistle, and whether the engineer blew it on purpose or because he was at the crossing I will never know.

I had the little Taylorcraft aircraft, and CF-BIE had no insulation on its fabric. The thin material didn't deaden the sound one bit—being right above the whistle was just like having your ear at the bell of a big horn. Anyhow, it was extremely loud. I was young at that time, only seventeen, and as my ticker was at its strongest it didn't stop ticking.

Fortunately, I survived that ordeal. Now I'll tell you about my last low-flying event. It hadn't been that many years since I was sitting in the old school house, and I remembered how sleepy it could get in there on a hot summer day. So I got the stupid idea of giving it a good buzzing.

I was flying my Tiger Moth—a real good, fully aerobatic aircraft. I started out on the dumb maneuver, flying just over the ground from the east, directly toward the school house. I intended to pull up quickly, about two hundred feet from the school, and wake them all up in there—give them all something to talk about. Well, given that I was flying as fast as the old moth would go, and the machine was twice as heavy as the Taylorcraft, which was only 800 lbs, the inertia took me closer to the school house than I intended to go. The old girl came up and cleared the roof, but not by nearly as much as I had intended to.

After I was up in the air and headed for home, it hit me like a ton of bricks that I had just done the craziest, dumbest, stupidest thing of my life, and that was the last time I flew low just for the heck of it.

CF-BIE – Taylorcraft: The first aircraft I purchased and flew – 1944.

CF-CSP – Tiger Moth: The next aircraft I bought and flew – 1945 – a fully aerobatic aircraft.

CHAPTER FIVE

Some Close Calls

After that fiasco with the school house, I became a much saner kind of flyer. I could be described as a very high flyer, which saved my bacon twice in my flying career.

I was in my Stinson Voyager 150. I had put in a very busy winter on skis in 46/47, and spent the summer of 1947 on floats. CF ELS had an aromatic hard black composite prop installed on it. They called it the prop with a brain, and it was a good description. Each blade had a counterweight attached to it on a short arm at the base of the hub of the prop. When this engine was stopped you could take the prop in your hands and freely flip the blades into fine or coarse pitch with zero resistance. Anyhow, the prop had put in a lot of flying time and it was worn out. I remember that near the end I could feel that the bearings were wearing out, but, always being short of time, it never got checked out and overhauled.

Later in the fall of '47, I was coming home at 8,000 or even maybe 10,000 feet, when all of a sudden the engine RPM zoomed up. I had to pull the throttle back as fast as I could or the engine might have flown apart. It was like a very short hailstorm when those round steel ball bearings hit the windshield—the prop went into the fine pitch, so even at a slow air speed, I couldn't use much power. The aircraft flew, though in a slow decline mode, but this was where being way up in the sky paid off. Even though I was about 60 miles from home, I just made it to our runway.

I'm sure Angel had a lot to do with that event. I was very sad to lose that prop; it had pulled me through a lot of times that any other prop wouldn't have. But they had quit making it already and you couldn't even get parts, so I was forced to say goodbye to an old friend and put on a traditional wooden prop made for 150 hp.

The next time things went wrong high in the sky was when a big mining company hired me to move their camp to another location, only a few miles from the first site. It was difficult because this was the most rugged terrain I had ever saw; the granite rock faces went straight up at the shoreline 40 to 50 feet, and I had to take off with heavy loads many times, just clearing the rock wall. The lake was small, making for a long day of "heart in the mouth" at every take off, and there were many trips, as the company only moved the camp a few miles.

Anyhow, we got the camp moved, and I was on my way home. Fortunately I was way up there in the sky when, all of a sudden, the engine began to run rough. I forget this detail but there must have been a big heavy bang, because the crankshaft had broken in two, right behind the main. Immediately, the oil pressure started to drop and the cylinder head temperature began to rise.

I had no idea what was going wrong; the only thing I can tell you now is that the crankshaft had broken in two pieces, but luckily it broke in a way that allowed the back piece of the crank to keep on turning. That's what the mags are fastened to, but the back piece slipped back a little. This retarded the timing, and everything was happening fast. I had no idea of what had happened, but in my wildest dreams I didn't consider that the crankshaft had broken. It's about 68 years ago, so I can't tell you how big that crank was, but it was a large one.

Anyway, all I could do was throttle right back to a low boost and RPM. As a result, I started losing altitude. I was still over Saskatchewan, but by coaxing the aircraft along and keeping the cylinder head temperature on the dial I was able to keep the aircraft flying and get to our base at Cold Lake.

Fortunately I was up high enough that I made it home without a forced landing. When I got back, L.D., my engineer, checked it all over and over from the outside. We still couldn't figure out what had gone wrong. After a couple of hours we started the engine up; it still ran rough, but the oil pressure wasn't too bad, so we decided to take her up for a test flight. We had just gotten up in the air, and were flying around the base when the engine temperature started to climb fast. The oil pressure was dropping just as quickly, so being just over the base I landed right away, and L.D. proceeded to dismantle the motor.

When he got to the main throw, there it was—the shaft, broken in two, but luckily it had broken jaggedly enough that it kept on turning the back end and the mags with it. I often had the thought: if that shaft had broken on any of those takeoffs from the camp with the big rock walls around it, and broken clean, then the engine would have stopped, I would have flown smack right into the rocks, and it would have been like swatting a fly against a wall. Clearly, I wouldn't be writing this story and book. So I'm giving my Angel an extra big thank you on this one. Triple thanks, Angel!

CF-ELS – Stinson Voyager: Four-place aircraft. The machine I flew into the North in 1946. Here I am wondering how we're going to get all these bags plus three people into this little plane, but we did.

CF-ELS on floats: Notice the bottom tail fin. It was put on because
the Stinson was a 108-2 model (the small-tail version).

CHAPTER SIX

Serious Flying

Now I'll tell you how and why I went north to make some money. It was the end of 1946 in the early winter. I had traded in the Taylorcraft and bought the Stinson, a 108-2 Voyager 4 place, 150 hp machine—a really good aircraft. I had been flying at Red Lake, Ontario, under a friend's charter, helping him out as he had a pretty good little business going. One time when I was on the way back to Portage, I had stopped at Aircraft Services Winnipeg and was sitting in the little coffee shop. A friend came by and sat down; we got talking and he told me, "You should be up north at Cold Lake"—at the time, it was a beehive of activity. Lynn Lake had just been discovered, and every mining exploration and mining company in the country was in Cold Lake, trying to get their people to the Lynn Lake area, which was about 100 miles directly north.

I was in the air early the next day. After a full day's flying, I made it to Flin Flon. I arrived at Cold Lake, a little place a mile away from Sherridon, Manitoba, where Sherrit Gordon Mining Co. had their operation's main office.

I was sick as a dog from not eating at all the day before, and eating the wrong kind of supper. I had $1.75 in my pocket. Talk about starting at the bottom, but I went over to Sherrit Gordon at Sherridon and told them I had arrived and was looking for business. They received me really well and gave me a trip to Lynn Lake the next day, along with $100.00. I was in business!

I was really busy from that day on. I flew all winter until spring break-up and made some good money—enough to put floats on the Stinson and rebuild the ribs on the bottom of the fuselage, which I had flattened to the frame.

The snow in the north was really deep that winter of 46/47. The lakes were well-covered. At most trappers' cabins, the trappers had a hardened path out from the cabin to the lake, with a hole in the ice where they could fish a little and get their drinking water. But my Stinson's skis were far too narrow for such conditions. They were made for airports and light snow. So what I had to do at these lakes was to taxi up to the trapper's hard trail and get the skis right on top. If I went too far, then the skis would slip down on the forward side and drop a couple of feet into the soft deep snow, and the belly would drag over the hard trail and flatten out the ribs a little more. So after a whole winter of this all, the ribs were flattened right level with the main frame.

The next summer an aircraft repair person had to cut back the fabric to weld on float fittings anyway, so it was a perfect time to fix the ribs and give the airplane a new look. I got the floats installed and docked the aircraft at a nice cement ramp into the Assiniboine River at Brandon Avenue, just to the east of a tall brewery. It was right at a bend in the river, and it was a challenge to have the aircraft in the air and banked to the right to stay over the water before we got to this brewery.

As soon as I got my pilot's license endorsed to float fly, I flew back to Cold Lake again. I was soon really busy again, and got a friend to come up north and help me out with making trips for the prospectors and trappers. We also flew a lot of fresh fish. I had tubs made up for that. We got so busy, I decided to rent an old STD Waco with no cowlings on the motor from an air charter company that was falling on hard times over in Prince Albert, Saskatchewan.

I'll never forget the episode that happened when I was checking out that old STD Waco. We were on the Saskatchewan River and the pilot was trying to get it up off the water, but it didn't want to go, and the high steel bridge to the west was getting closer and closer. Finally he got off the water, but I'm sure we came close enough to trade paint jobs between the top of that bridge and the bottom of the floats. I'm positive Angel had a finger in the pie during that fiasco—thanks once again, Angel, for helping us get over that bridge.

I flew the Waco back to Cold Lake and we put in the rest of the summer—busy, busy. At freeze-up we flew the Waco back to North Battleford. I took a picture of that trip; you can see the smoke stack at Flin Flon in the distance to the northwest.

That winter, 1947/48, I purchased CF-AYQ, another STD Waco about the same age as the one I had rented. But this airplane was in excellent shape. It had just undergone a renovation, and it had a 240 hp, Jacob's L4 cowlings and all. So we put the winter in, busier than ever, until next spring at breakup when it wasn't possible fly because all the snow and ice was melting.

Towaganac Exploration Mining Co. of Toronto just finished a major overhaul of CF-BDU, a custom Waco they had been flying since day one, around the time when I first started up. And it was for sale. They had their base right almost beside ours, so I knew the aircraft well. Intending to purchase it for $12,000, I took the train to Toronto, which was a two-day trip. I slept almost all the way—two days sleep was about what I needed to catch up on my rest. So it worked out well.

I arrived in Toronto and checked out the BDU. They had done a thorough job; it was just like a brand new aircraft. I gladly gave them the $12,000, and as I had done so much float time already I didn't need any checkout on it. I just filled the fuel tanks up brim-full and started my takeoff run.

Well, it's a good thing that Toronto has a large lake. I had no problem getting on the step, but do you think I could get the old girl to lift off the water? It stuck onto that lake surface. I tried everything I had learned up to that point to break its seal to the surface of the water. Every float plane has a different feel or characteristic as to how it has to be treated to get it to break loose. Finally, after a long, long run she lifted off the water, and off we went to Sudbury. The liftoff wasn't spectacular, but I was starting to understand how the old girl liked to be treated.

I have to tell you about the problem that I had at the Sudbury fuel stop, though. When Towaganac over-hauled the motor, they forgot to put a stopper on the end of the dipstick chain to prevent it from getting lost. In Sudbury, the chain just ran off the tank and fell into six feet of water. I didn't know what I was going to do—the water was ice cold, and there was even still some ice on the lake. There were a few young guys close by, to whom I offered $20.00 to go in and get it, but no dice. I had to do it myself. I was still shaking like a leaf fifty miles later. Man, that was an experience that will never leave my memory.

The next fuel stop was Geraldton, Ontario. I arrived there and my heart sank at the sight: a very small lake, much smaller than what I had required so far to lift off the surface. But what could I do other than to set the aircraft down and learn very, very fast? What a guy has to do in this flying game is unreal. I'm sure it was Angel that got me out of that lake. Many, many thanks for getting me out of that situation!

I finally learned a way to "twist" the floats out of the water. It was a very unique feel I got right in the seat of my pants while I was up on the step. As I was skimming along really fast on the water, just as I got that feeling, I figured out how to gently twist out.

My fourth aircraft was a CF-AYQ – Standard Waco: Here the floats are being installed.

Here's CF-BDU – Custom Waco 330 HP: The float plane I purchased
from Toronto and flew back to Cold Lake in 1948.

CF-BDU on floats: A powerful, good airplane for bush operation.
It had a constant-speed 9'3" steel prop installed.

CF-BDU on skis ready to go. Notice the shock absorber on the ski pedestal. Worked very well.

A rare occasion as all three of our float planes are at the dock at one time.
CF-BDU custom Waco, CF-AYQ standard Waco and CF-ELS Stinson.

This is CF-AYQ, outfitted with a Jacobs L4 motor, the second aircraft to be added to Bowes Airways. We operated out of Cold Lake, Manitoba in 1948. This plane was a good workhorse for bush flying.

We're returning the Waco that I had rented to North Battleford. Notice the smoke from the big smoke stack at Flin Flon at the top of the picture.

CHAPTER SEVEN

Wilderness Hospitality and Perils

With lots of practice, I learned to get big loads off the water. I flew a lot of trips and hauled a lot of fish pretty well all summer, some trout and jumbo whites. Now that white fish is a great fish to eat. It's a little mellower than pickerel, which itself is mellower than trout. But it seems to be a little meatier than pickerel. On a day-to-day basis, it's a beautiful fish to eat and we ate it steadily—it's the staple food of the north.

One time, bad weather forced me down for about two days and I stayed with an old trapper who, with his wife, was living in this cabin. They were out of food. The Bombardier that was supposed to show up with their supplies hadn't appeared yet. I think the trapper's wife had flour and maybe something else, but they were right down to the wire.

Well, the day I stayed there, she cooked us four meals: breakfast, dinner, supper and bedtime snack. All she really had to work with was fish, and I'll never forget how delicious all of the meals were; she did the fish four ways, all of them good. Before I finally left for home they made me promise to find that Bombardier and make sure their supplies came to them pronto. They were really nice people.

On the second day the bad weather had let up a little, and I had a passenger with me on that trip, so I thought I'd give it a whirl and see what it was like to fly home. Well, I got in the air, but it was still bad. I turned back as fast as I could with my tail between my legs, got back to that cabin, and waited the weather out until it cleared up. I'm sure Angel was in there keeping a finger on the situation from start to finish—thanks!

It's about the right time to tell you about South Indian Lake. I would say this place played the biggest role in my life in the north after, of course, Cold Lake, where I was living and had my base of operations. After flying in to South Indian settlement I met a fur trader and his wife. We became very good friends. I started going up there on a frequent basis. It was about halfway to Churchill, and almost on the same line of flight. I got to know him as he was the main free trader at South Indian. He started to give me more and more freight, though I didn't get it all. He would save a little for another company, who had been serving him for years. I will never forget hearing their lament through the grapevine later—they said that a young whippersnapper from Portage la Prairie had stolen the business out of South Indian, and they were not impressed.

I stayed at the trader's house many times, and I still remember the great coffee his wife made. She had a unique way of doing it. I've tried it myself but it's never turned out like hers. What she did was bring the water and coffee to a fierce boil, throw in a dash of cold water, let it sit for a few minutes, and then pour you a cup. The best coffee I've ever drank. It must have been the pure lake water she was using that made it so unique.

South Indian Lake makes me recollect the scariest forced landing experience of all. I had purchased an Anson V in the fall and I was flying fish, mostly pickerel, and would that old girl ever take a load. I just called it "old," but really it was almost a new airplane. I bought it from war assets—they were selling them out of Carberry's former air force base. I had to make it airworthy and get skis installed, so while this was getting done, I took my twin engine training and got my pilot's license endorsed for twin engine flying in Winnipeg.

I was ready to take the Anson north when sad story came in. Some big mining company had purchased an Anson V like mine, and three weeks earlier, taken it up to Cold Lake too. They had hired a fellow who had flown the custom Waco that I had purchased the year before. Now in all my flying days, of all the pilots I ever met, I never knew a pilot more cautious and safe than this one. But he had just flown his Anson up to Cold Lake about three weeks before, crashed it, and was killed.

Talk about hard to believe. The finest, most careful pilot I had ever known, crashed and killed in exactly the same kind of aircraft I was about to fly north to the same place. Here I was, a young 23-year-old pilot with a fraction of the experience that he had, and he was suddenly dead.

It was a pretty tough decision, but I had no other choice. I just had to go, but by dotting my i's and crossing my t's, everything turned out OK with the Anson V; I should add, it was the nicest airplane to handle and best I've ever flown. Two 450 hp Wasp junior motors, and the airplane was all wood construction—just like the Mosquito fighter/bomber, which I never owned but consider to be the greatest prop aircraft ever built.

The Anson's motors are so good, I have been told that when the engine is overhauled it is in perfect shape, like you could put it together again with no new parts. When you get two of them running side by side you have 900 hp—lots of power, and smooth as silk. A beautiful aircraft to fly.

Anyhow, I took on a heavy load of fresh pickerel from South Indian Lake and headed for Cold Lake. Just about halfway home I ran into heavy snow, so I got down on to the tree tops. I had made that trip back and forth so many times that I knew it like the back of my hand. I knew a small lake was just ahead and if my line of flight stayed on the same heading I should hit it dead on—and it worked out that way.

But once I got over the lake I had to bank to the left and into an extremely tight 90° turn to keep the lake in my sight. It was a small lake and if I lost it, being right at the tree tops I would have been in big trouble. I had a heavy load of fish and I'd had to load it as far forward as possible. The Anson liked to have the centre of gravity just behind the main wing-spar. If further back, the aircraft would go into a speed stall in a tight turn like I was doing.

Right in the middle of the maneuver, the whole airplane shuddered. It was decision time for the Anson: to either keep swinging the tail around faster than the front end was going, or give in to the two Wasp Juniors that were giving all they could.

I had already pushed the throttle through the gates as far ahead as possible, and then came the best feeling I've ever experienced: the motors won out, and I could feel a new power pulling us ahead. The nose went down and the tail came up. We started flying again! A thousand thanks, Angel; I really needed help with that one.

I could still see the lake shoreline out my window, so I turned west into the wind and started landing on the lake. As the snow was really deep, I had to make a circle in it, going round and round until I had a packed trail. I left the aircraft on this trail facing west, close to the east shoreline. Now came the job of putting on the big wing covers and diluting the oil so the engines would turn over in the morning and start. It was a long night. I don't think I slept a wink.

The timber wolves were close by—really close. They sounded like they were at the door. I was tempted to open the door a crack, but wasn't brave enough. They could smell all the fresh fish. I remember starting the blowpot up once in a while to warm up the air in the plane so the fish would not freeze. I had to be really careful not to run the pot too long, as it was using up the oxygen and creating monoxide, which made the air very toxic. I could have gassed myself very easily.

Finally morning came, and with it, two problems that needed solving to get that big ship out of there. The first thing I had to do was clear the snow to the ice in a fairly wide path in front of both skis for about 30 feet. I had to shovel the snow under each ski from the front as far under as I dare. My plan was to raise the tail up with the propwash and bang down the fuselage. Now, the fuselage was made in three sections bolted together, each constructed from 1/8" plywood. To jar the aircraft loose would require a severe jolt, but it had to be gentle enough to avoid breaking the airplane in two.

Don't forget about that big load of fish that contributed to the strain put on that fuselage. My Mark V Anson had an engine crankcase oil gas dilution system, allowing you to bring gas into the oil while it was running. As a result, the motors were nice and loose the next morning for starting. It was a really smart system.

After removing all the wing covers, engine tents, and so on, I was ready to take off from this little lake. The engines started up nicely, so after a run up I was ready to execute my plan to get the plane moving. I revved the engines until there was enough propwash to get the tail up to flight level, which was about six feet high in the air from the ice level.

I had shoveled the snow down to the ice ahead the skis far enough under each ski to leave a pedestal of snow under each one. The snow was hard and the skis held up as the temp was 30 – 40 degrees out. It was cold!

Everything was good so far, so I dropped the tail hard; the jolt broke down the snow pedestal—it worked!—and the skis fell to the bare ice, and she started moving forward with full power on. The skis slid along the bare ice paths I had made, so by the time the skis had slid into the snow, the hard ice surface had cleaned them off, and the aircraft was picking up speed fast. As the two 450 hp Wasp Junior motors hummed and purred, we headed for home.

Now the next problem: after all of this engine-running time, I was getting low on fuel. This meant that the aircraft was lighter, which could have been a factor in the machine getting off that small lake and clearing the trees on the shore line, so I was happy about that. But the indicator was dropping by the minute, so I made a beeline for home, right on the flight path so as not to waste any fuel, and made it right to the Fish Dock. Near the end our propellers stopped turning; our fuel had run out, but we were home, and mostly because of Angel's influence—I'm positive this was the big reason for the success of the whole operation. Thanks, thanks again to you, Angel.

One last comment about the experience of speed stalls in a tight turn: I believe this might be what happened to that Anson V that went north three weeks before I did and crashed, killing the pilot.

My MARK V ANSON 900HP! I flew fish with it in the winter of 1948-1949.
It was a beautiful airplane to fly, with all-wood construction.

One cold, cold morning after I had storm-stayed with these good people overnight, my blow pot
would not go. These fellows took their little tin stove, chimney pipes and all out of their cabin;
then we put it in the tent under the motor. It heated the motor up fine. This operation
shows that attitude and mindset can overcome a language barrier—a lesson for us all.

CHAPTER EIGHT

Learning the Hard Way

My first winter piloting, in 1946/47, I was bush flying in the north. I learned the dos and don'ts as I went—one of the first lessons was to know the aircraft's load capacity limits. I had to pick up a trapper, a prospector and his big dog, and his bigger packsack, which I'm sure was heavier than a man. I was definitely at the beginning of the learning curve.

Amazingly, we got everything into the airplane, including the big bag and dog. I could barely see the prospector sitting beside me, as he had so many things on his lap. I might add, those prospectors always had a bag of rock samples as well, which would turn out to be as heavy as an anvil.

The underlying problem was that we were on a small lake. I blasted off toward the north on takeoff. Well, the 150 hp Franklin and the aerometric prop, the one with the brain, did their best, but the north shoreline was coming up really fast. The Stinson skis cleared the ice, but the trees were right there and I was going right into them!

I still didn't have much flying speed, but I had no choice other than to turn sharp to the right just before I came to the treeline. I was in a 90° turn, the wings were almost perpendicular to the ground, and the fuselage was on its side and pointing towards the sky. This airplane felt like it was hanging in the air, with the prop holding it up there—our air speed was very slow, stalling speed, but the Stinson had stall-proof wing slats.

There we were, pointing toward the sky at almost 45°. The trapper sitting in the passenger seat later told me that he was watching out his window at the wing tip that was almost scraping the ice, scared stiff that it would catch the ground. But the little Stinson and prop kept us hanging in the air. The skis weren't too far away from the trees, but the little Stinson finally gained enough air speed to let us get above the treetops and start flying normally again. So with a lot of help from Angel once again, we pulled through that narrow scrape and I learned a lesson the hard way. They say that's the way you really learn—and boy did I learn that one, Again, more thanks Angel!

I learned another lesson from the ice on an even smaller lake. I was landing and I touched down on glare ice. It was just like it would be if you had skates on—the Stinson had come with nice skis, but they were made for airport flying, very narrow, only eight inches wide, and the ski was round crossways as well as lengthways—kind of shaped like a longer, flatter spoon. It felt like we were going to coast forever, and the trees on the far side of the lake were getting closer and closer. I had to get stopped—and quick—before crashing into the trees on the north shore. You won't believe it, but I pushed the throttle forward, which created the needed propulsion to blast on the rudder. At the same time I put the left rudder on full and used the propwash to spin the aircraft around 180°, so in an instant she was sliding on the ice going backwards, like a car in reverse. I then gave the motor full throttle and this braking effect brought the aircraft to a stop just in time to avoid hitting the bush. Whew! Anyhow, that's what is known as a ground loop, with a much wiser guy behind the controls and another rescue by Angel—many thanks, Angel!

Learning to fly on floats. Brandon Ave, Winnipeg. On the Assiniboine River – 1947.
Notice that aeromatic "prop with the brain." It saved my neck many times.

Bowes Airways dock at Cold Lake 1948. We were fortunate to be in a nice sheltered bay in the lake.

CHAPTER NINE

A Human Touch

I've told you about bad weather and narrow scrapes, but we had some interesting personal encounters, too, once in a while. One summer night, L.D., my mechanic, and I decided to take a couple of girls on a small trip to a lake about twenty miles south of Cold Lake. So we did, but at about 3:00 am in the morning I noticed the sky getting very dark back to the west. It didn't look good at all so I took the custom Waco CF-BDU off for home. I had just gotten up in the air when L.D., who had been sleeping on the floor behind the pilot's seat, came up at my right arm and burst out, loud and clear, "Holy cow!" as he caught sight of that black wall to the west. By this time we were up about 500 feet and headed straight toward home base, which was pretty well due north.

The sky to the west was something I had never seen before or since. It was pitch black and was as menacing as imaginable, and just a perfect wall directly ahead of us. We were flying right alongside the wall, which was quite a scary sight. But we flew tight along the wall and landed at the base in a few minutes. We hadn't gone very far from home, but we had landed just in time when the storm hit. It seems like Angel never had a break those days.

Another recreational trip, I guess you'd call it, was when L.D. and I decided to head down to The Pas one Saturday night. There was going to be a big dance at the hotel, and we were looking forward to it. Maybe we would run across some girls from the town. We were having supper in the big dining room restaurant and L.D. was sitting on the other side of the room. I wanted to get his attention for something, so I stood up and yelled across the room, "L.D.!"

Well, a small, wizened old guy at the end of the room jumped up and hollered back, "Algiers, I was there." It came across really hilariously; the whole place went into an uproar.

After supper in the hotel room, somebody brought out a big bottle of Navy rum. That sure tasted good—I don't know if you have ever had your share of Dark Navy rum, but when it hits you, you're out like a light. As a result, I slept through the whole dance. The boys woke me up after the dance was over and told me how good it was, kind of rubbing in the fact that I missed it all. But thinking about it later, I told myself I was probably better off having a long siesta. I could have gotten into trouble at the dance, so maybe Angel knew best and managed things accordingly.

In the summer of 1947, the Indian Department hired me to fly to York Factory to pick up a mother and a sick baby and fly them to The Pas Hospital. When I arrived I noticed an ocean freighter ship just sitting out where the mighty Nelson River empties into Hudson Bay. They said it had been out there for years, stuck in the silt that had been dumped into the bay by the Nelson. Port Nelson's inhabitants eventually abandoned it and established the Port of Churchill at the outlet of the Saskatchewan River, further north on Hudson Bay. Keeping ahead of the Nelson River turned out to be impossible—it brought in silt and mud faster than it could be dredged out. They had already built a long row of two-storey buildings, painted white. From the air you could see this row of buildings for miles.

Now let me tell you how that immense Nelson fooled me, just like it did the old timers when they tried to build a port there. The huge amount of water that is thrust into the bay causes a movement in the water that is not noticeable at the surface because of the waves. But at the point where I untied the Stinson the water was moving outward from the shore, along with a slight breeze. I was out in the bay moving backwards.

Anyhow, the problem was the battery was dead, and the motor wouldn't start. To pull the prop, I had to swing myself under the wing strut. So my eyes were down, nearly at sea level. Every time I went out to pull the prop, I noticed the tail dipping closer to the waves. I had the control wheel pulled all the way back, and got the mother to hold it right back hard as she could. She was also holding her baby tightly in her arms while doing this. The airplane was moving backwards fairly fast now, as the offshore breeze was getting stronger, along with the offshore undercurrent. If the tail had touched the waves, it would have been sucked down into the water quickly. We would have been submerged upside down, and no doubt all three of us would have drowned immediately.

Needless to say, I was probably the most desperate person in existence for a long way in any direction. On that final trip to the prop, with that final heave, the engine started. That was the sweetest sound I've ever heard. I got behind the wheel and off of that choppy bay. When we got on course to Gillam and were flying safely, I looked over at the mother holding her baby as tightly as ever. I can't speak a word of Cree and she didn't speak English, but we both had a smile ear to ear, and that said it all. Once again, a million thanks, Angel, for saving us!

Red was my faithful partner for 17 years less a month and 2 days – June 1, 1997, to April 28, 2014.
Nothing in this world can match a good dog's bond. My last Stinson CF-HZM is behind my truck.

Red, my loyal and faithful partner, lying on the seat of my '94
Chevy half-ton, always at my side like a true pal and partner.

Here's Red's photo again.

CHAPTER TEN

Back on the Ground

When I got back down south, after selling my aircraft and business to another company, Dad had lined up a good cash-earning job with the Prairie Farm Rehabilitation Act. They decided to re-build the dyke on the north side of the river from Poplar Point to Portage. They gave another outfit the east half and I had the west half. I built an 8 x 16 little trailer to live in while on the job, and a high boy trailer to haul the bulldozer. I had never built a trailer before but it turned out OK and hauled many a caterpillar on it, with a brush cutter even—that was a big load, but it did it.

The next thing I had to build was a super heavy 2/24 breaking plow. That was a two-year project because it was very heavy duty and strong. I used a 6 x 6 heavy box for the main frame, three TD-18 bottom rollers for hubs and bearings, and old threshing machine steel wheel rims filled in with 3/8 steel plate for the wheels. It took two cats, a D8 and D7 or TD-18 to pull the plow. But it would slice the biggest of stumps and turn them out of the ground with a loud crunch.

The most harrowing experience I had personally was when a TD-18 hydraulic hose burst. On extremely hot summer days the oil would come to a boil and shoot out of a relief valve on the hyd tank on a steady basis. One day, I was working the system pretty hard and a one-inch hose that was feeding a big eight-inch hydraulic cylinder broke; the broken hose shot the oil full force right on my bare back.

The foreman on the job was an old farmer. I was stumbling around—I was in shock and didn't know what to do—but this wise old guy did the right thing. He ordered me to lay face down on the ground, and he took dirt which was all loose from the bulldozer and he covered my back over with it. The doctor later said that was the best thing he could have done, because the raw skin that had been blistered by the boiling oil healed perfectly. He got the dirt on so fast that my back healed in good time, without a single scar.

It's amazing what those old timers know about that kind of injury. Again, thanks to Angel for having someone on hand who would know what to do. I'm sure you could have asked a lot of people in the world before finding one with the right kind of knowledge, but Angel had him ready. A thousand thanks again, Angel!

Another important event happened later on that summer or fall. We were working alongside a half dozen other machines on a big diversion dam on the Assiniboine River, just east of Portage la Prairie and north of the old "whoop and holler" (the former site of a dance hall where everyone in the area used to go for a fun night out). Anyhow, our job was to push dirt out into the water to create the eventual dam or dyke that would be closing off the loop in the river. We were working twenty-four hour days. The scrapers would leave dirt at the base of the dam going out into the river. We would back up behind this dirt and push it out and over the edge off this protruding dam into the river. By the third day we had created quite an impressive structure. We were nearly a third of the way across the river.

One night, at about 4:00 AM in the morning, the foreman on the shift came excitedly and knocked on our little trailer door and blustered out that I needed to come down to the job right away: my TD-18 bulldozer was in the river!

Sure enough, the operator had gone to sleep and drove right over the end of the dam. The roar of the river and rushing water was very scary. There, with the back end sticking out of the river at an angle, was my TD-18. The dozer blade was right in the muck at the river bottom, and half of the cat was in the river.

As for the task of pulling it out of the river, they started out with a couple of D8 cats pulling it, which didn't have the slightest effect. Next a third was added on, which still didn't budge it at all, as the dozer blade was acting like a big suction cup on the river bottom. When a fourth was moved in, it still wouldn't come out.

At this point, they decided to bulldoze the dam right into the river and down to the same level as the TD-18. All that work building the dam and they just pushed it into the river. However, even with three or four machines pulling it, the cat still wouldn't come out of the river bed. So they hooked up all five cats and things started to happen.

First, the machine started moving. Our cat was straight down so all the machines were actually pulling down on its hitch. You should have seen the size of those big cables pulling, all hooked to the hitch. The result was that they pulled the hitch right off of the main frame, shearing all six one-inch studs clean off the main body of the cat. All that was left was the big drawbar which is pinned underneath the cat's main frame, and by this time it had been pulled away from the body. Though not solidly connected anymore, the large pin holding it to the main frame hung on, and our TD-18 finally came out of the muck.

You should have seen that drawbar, twisted like a propeller and bowed like a banana, only worse. I hate to think about what that operation cost, but they were sure good to me about it. I was never told how much it cost—it had to be very high, plus all that work destroyed. Even though I hadn't been driving I was worried that they would try to recoup some of the costs of the rescue operation from me, as the owner of the troublesome machine, but I was never asked for a penny. Thanks to somebody somewhere, maybe Angel.

Still, I sure had a job on my hands getting that machine operational again. All six studs had been broken out of the main frame. I got the blacksmith to straighten the drawbar out. That guy put in a full day stirring his forge. He and the drawbar were red hot, then he started pounding it, and would you believe it, the old guy got it straight enough that we were able to put it back on the cat and use it. Angel did a great job of resolving an extremely trying situation. Thanks again, my Angel, thanks.

CHAPTER ELEVEN

Final Thoughts

I should tell you how I got dubbed "the Flying Kid." The Winnipeg Tribune had sent a reporter up to Sherridon to get stories about the Lynn Lake rush. I happened to be in the Cambrian Hotel beer parlour to drum up business—I wasn't drinking beer, as my stomach won't accept the stuff—another thing I was blessed with. Anyhow, the reporter was there too, trying to get stories for the Tribune. He came over to my table, being a reporter and full of questions. When we finished talking two hours later, I thought by now he probably knew more about me than I did myself. The next week a big story came out in the Winnipeg Tribune about the "Flying Kid," and that's how that tag got started. I know one thing: good came out of the article. It sure gained me a lot of business. I couldn't have bought that kind of publicity. The "Flying Kid" was a handle that has stayed with me, and that is why I'm using it now.

Remember how that train whistle blasted me when I was flying directly above the rails? Well, if I heard a sound like that now it would be game over, since, as the doctors say, my heart (or what is left of it) can only fulfill about 20% of the usual pumping function. The left ventricle muscles have died, and sadly they can never be revived. In 2016 I was hospitalized three times and diagnosed with severe heart problems, but I'm feeling better now. I'm minimizing and tidying my personal things up, and jotting down these tales as I remember them. I finally had to retire due to my health problems, giving me time to write. Most of the stories show how Angel was with me all the way, pulling me through countless times—otherwise I wouldn't still be here.

So I'm going to wrap this book up there. Thank you very, very much if you are still with me. I hope you found it interesting. This is something that my family has been after me to do for years. So bye for now, and thanks again.

Yours truly,
Keith Bowes, "The Flying Kid"

Pals.